LANDMARKS
INSTRUCTIONS

1 Open the front flap on the VR viewer. Bring the top and side flaps up and over. The slide flaps attach to the side of the viewer with Velcro.

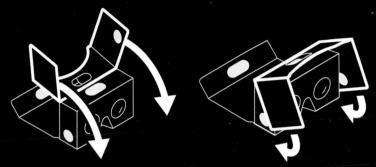

2 Download PI VR Landmarks, available on the App Store or Google Play. Direct links to the store locations are found at: pilbooks.com/PIVRLandmarks.

3 Launch the app. You may be asked to calibrate your viewer by scanning the QR code found on the bottom of the viewer itself. You will be able to change your viewer settings later in the options menu.

4 After calibrating your viewer, you will be prompted to scan the QR code found to the right to verify your possession of this book.

5 You will see a double image of an interactive map with 10 landmarks on your phone. Insert your smartphone into the front compartment of the VR viewer. The line between the two images should line up with the notch at the center point of the viewer, between the two lenses. If your screen seems blurry, make sure the smartphone is aligned precisely with the center of the viewer. Adjusting the phone left or right a few millimeters can make a big difference. The tilt of the viewer and the phone can also affect how the screen looks to you.

6 Look around to explore! PI VR Landmarks does not require a lever or remote control. You control each interaction with your gaze. When you see a loading circle, keep your gaze focused until it loads fully to access videos, slideshows, and games.

Loading

7 Gaze at the X to close out of video, slideshow, or game screens.

pil
Publications International, Ltd.

Get the App!

This book is enhanced by an app that can be downloaded from the App Store or Google Play*. Apps are available to download at no cost. Once you've downloaded the app to your smartphone**, use the QR code found on page 1 of this book to access an immersive, 360° virtual reality environment. Then slide the phone into the VR viewer and you're ready to go.

Compatible Operating Systems

- Android 4.1 (JellyBean) or later

- iOS 8.0 or later

Compatible Phones

The app is designed to work with smartphones with a screen size of up to 6 inches. Removing your device from its case may provide a better fit in the viewer. If your smartphone meets the above operating system requirements and has gyroscope functionality it should support GoogleVR. Publications International, Ltd. has developed and tested this software with the following devices:

- Google Nexus 5, Google Nexus 5X, Google Nexus 6P, Google Pixel

- Apple iPhone 6, Apple iPhone 6S, Apple iPhone 6 Plus, Apple iPhone 6S Plus, Apple iPhone 7, Apple iPhone 7 Plus

- Samsung Galaxy S5, Samsung Galaxy S5 Active, Samsung Galaxy S5 Sport, Samsung Galaxy S6, Samsung Galaxy S6 edge, Samsung Galaxy S6 edge +, Samsung Galaxy Note 4, Samsung Galaxy Note edge, Samsung Galaxy S7, Samsung Galaxy S7 edge, Samsung Galaxy Note 5, Samsung Galaxy S8

Caution

The viewer should not be exposed to moisture or extreme temperatures. The viewer is not water resistant. It is potentially combustible if the lenses are left facing a strong light source.

Apple, the Apple logo and iPhone are trademarks of Apple Inc., registered in the U.S. and other countries. App Store is a service mark of Apple Inc., registered in the U.S. and other countries. Google Play and the Google Play logo are trademarks of Google Inc. Nexus and Pixel are trademarks of Google Inc. Samsung, Galaxy and Galaxy Note are trademarks of Samsung Electronics Co. Ltd.

Cover art from Shutterstock.com

Interior art from Shutterstock.com

App content from Encyclopædia Britannica, Inc., Filament Games, and Shutterstock.com

Louis Weber, CEO
Publications International, Ltd.
8140 Lehigh Avenue
Morton Grove, IL 60053

Permission is never granted for commercial purposes.

 Publications International, Ltd.

For inquiries email: customer_service@pubint.com

ISBN: 978-1-68022-953-0

Manufactured in China.

8 7 6 5 4 3 2 1

*We reserve the right to terminate the apps.
**Smartphone not included. Standard data rates may apply to download. Once downloaded, the app does not use data or require wifi access.

CONTENTS

INTRODUCTION

Landmarks are features of the land or structures that are notable or unique. The first section of this book highlights a selection of natural landmarks. Some natural landmarks are so impressive that in order to ensure that they are preserved for generations to come, they are protected in national parks.

The second section of this book includes information about human-made landmarks—notable buildings, monuments, bridges, canals, and other structures that were built by people. These can include recent feats of engineering as well as the remains of ancient cities and architecture.

NATIONAL PARKS

Every nation has areas of natural beauty. These areas almost always contain valuable and interesting plants and animals that often cannot be found anywhere else on Earth. Therefore, these areas must be protected if they are to continue to add to society's enjoyment and scientific knowledge.

For this purpose dozens of countries in North and South America, Europe, Asia, Africa, Australia, and the South Pacific have established more than 3,500 national parks and other protected areas. Included in these are many nature reserves that have been set aside to conserve a particular kind of plant or animal. A number of countries have also set aside areas or sites of great historical significance.

A geyser at Yellowstone National Park.

ARCHAEOLOGY

The field of study called archaeology combines the excitement of treasure hunting with the investigative labor of detective work. Archaeology is the scientific study of the material remains of humankind's past. Its discoveries are the principal source of knowledge about prehistoric cultures.

The materials of archaeological study are both the things made by people and the things used by them. All the things fashioned by people—including settlements, buildings, tools, weapons, objects of ornament, and pure art—are called artifacts.

An archaeological excavation in Spain.

USE THE VR VIEWER AND ASSOCIATED APP!

Enhance your experience by using the app! Put your smartphone in the VR viewer and you'll be able to get a better view of ten landmarks from around the world: Burj Khalifa (United Arab Emirates), the Great Pyramid at Giza (Egypt), the Cathedral in Brasília (Brazil), the Leaning Tower of Pisa (Italy), Willis Tower (United States), Pyramid IV in the ruins of Tikal (Guatemala), Hagia Sophia (Turkey), the Sydney Opera House (Australia), the Taj Mahal (India), and the U.S. Capitol Building (United States). See video, images, animations, and more!

NATURAL WONDERS: NORTH AMERICA

DENALI

The highest mountain in North America, Denali (also called Mount McKinley) is located in south-central Alaska near the center of the Alaska Range. It rises 20,320 feet (6,194 meters) above sea level and 17,000 feet (5,200 meters) above the timberline.

NIAGARA FALLS

Situated between the U.S. state of New York and the Canadian province of Ontario, Niagara Falls is one of the most spectacular natural wonders on the North American continent. Every minute about 12,000,000 cubic feet (340,000 cubic meters), or 379,000 tons, of water pours in torrents over the cliffs of the falls of Niagara.

GREAT SMOKY MOUNTAINS

The Great Smoky Mountains, in Tennessee and North Carolina, are the highest of the ranges in the Appalachian system. The rocks exposed in the Great Smoky Mountains are among the oldest in the world. Botanists consider the region to be the original home of present-day Eastern vegetation. Almost untouched by human beings, with abundant rainfall of nearly 100 inches (254 centimeters) in a year and fertile soil, the area's plant life has developed in greater variety than anywhere else in the temperate zone.

About 150 species of trees have been found in the Great Smoky Mountains. (All of Europe has fewer than 100.)

GRAND CANYON

Nature's greatest example of sculpture, the Grand Canyon in northern Arizona is the most spectacular canyon in the world. It is a 277-mile (446-kilometer) gorge cut through high plateaus by the Colorado River. Within the walls of the canyon stand imposing peaks, canyons, and ravines. In general, the color of the canyon is red, but each stratum (a layer of the Earth) or group of strata has a distinctive hue—buff and gray, delicate green and pink, and, in its depths, brown, slate-gray, and violet.

No other place on Earth compares with the mile-deep Grand Canyon for its record of geological events. Some of the canyon's rocks date back about 4 billion years.

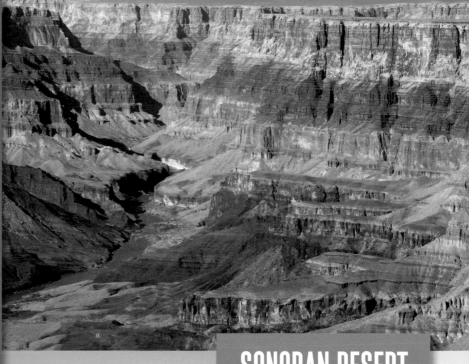

SONORAN DESERT

The Sonoran Desert is a hot, dry area in the Southwest region of the United States and in northwestern Mexico. It covers an area of 120,000 square miles (310,800 square kilometers). The vegetation of the Sonoran Desert is the most diverse of all the North American deserts. The saguaro cactus is the signature plant of the desert.

POPOCATÉPETL

The perpetually snowcapped, symmetrical cone of the Mexican volcano Popocatépetl rises to a height of 17,887 feet (5,452 meters). After lying inactive for more than 50 years, Popocatépetl erupted in December 1994, causing an ashfall over Puebla. Since then, volcanic activity has recurred sporadically.

Popocatépetl means "Smoking Mountain" in Nahuatl, a Meso-American Indian language.

AMERICA'S NATIONAL PARKS

In 1872 the United States government established Yellowstone National Park. It was the first national park in the world. Today every citizen of the United States shares in the ownership of the towering mountain peaks, gigantic canyons, and lush forests of the national parks.

Double Arch.

ARCHES

Arches National Park, in eastern Utah, is named after its spectacular red sandstone arches. There are more than 2,000 natural arches in the park, in addition to towers, mazes, and other massive rock formations.

Mesquite Flat Sand Dunes in Death Valley National Park.

DEATH VALLEY

The lowest point in the Western Hemisphere, Death Valley is also famous as a scene of suffering in the gold rush of 1849. There many gold seekers nearly lost their lives in searing heat. They gave the valley its grim name. The scorching heat has reached 134°F (57°C). Despite this heat, more than 600 kinds of plants thrive there.

EVERGLADES

Everglades National Park in southern Florida is a large natural area encompassing the southwestern portion of the larger Everglades region. The park, at 2,410 square miles (6,240 square kilometers), constitutes the largest subtropical wilderness left in the United States.

MAMMOTH CAVE

The longest cave system in the world is preserved at Mammoth Cave National Park in west-central Kentucky. The explored and mapped underground passages of the multilevel system have a combined length of more than 345 miles (555 kilometers). The caves lie within layers of limestone that go hundreds of feet underground.

SEQUOIA NATIONAL PARK

Sequoia National Park, a forested area in east-central California, was established in 1890 to protect groves of big trees, or giant sequoias *(Sequoiadendron giganteum)*. These trees are among the world's largest and oldest living things. The largest big tree in the park is known as the General Sherman Tree, which is thought to be 2,300 to 2,700 years old.

YELLOWSTONE

Yellowstone National Park is located principally in northwestern Wyoming and partly in southern Montana and eastern Idaho. Yellowstone's principal attractions are its some 10,000 hydrothermal features, which constitute roughly half of all those known in the world. The region's deeply fractured crust allows groundwater to seep down to where it makes contact with underlying magma. The superheated and mineral-rich water then returns to the surface as steam vents, fumaroles, colorful hot pools, mud cauldrons, paint pots, hot springs and terraces, hot rivers, and geysers.

NATURAL WONDERS:
SOUTH AMERICA

THE ANDES AND MOUNT ACONCAGUA

The giant Andean system, which is the longest mountain chain in the world, stretches along the entire western side of South America, a distance of about 5,500 miles (8,900 kilometers). In elevation it is exceeded only by the Himalayas in central Asia. The tallest peak is Mount Aconcagua, 22,831 feet (6,959 meters). Located on the border between Chile and Argentina, Aconcagua is the highest mountain in the Western Hemisphere.

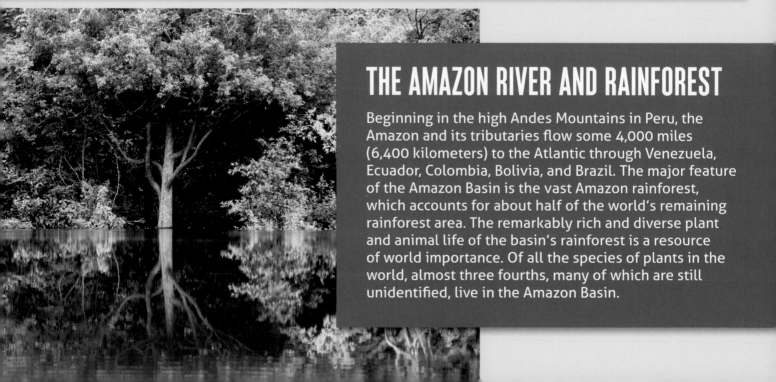

THE AMAZON RIVER AND RAINFOREST

Beginning in the high Andes Mountains in Peru, the Amazon and its tributaries flow some 4,000 miles (6,400 kilometers) to the Atlantic through Venezuela, Ecuador, Colombia, Bolivia, and Brazil. The major feature of the Amazon Basin is the vast Amazon rainforest, which accounts for about half of the world's remaining rainforest area. The remarkably rich and diverse plant and animal life of the basin's rainforest is a resource of world importance. Of all the species of plants in the world, almost three fourths, many of which are still unidentified, live in the Amazon Basin.

ANGEL FALLS

The highest waterfall in the world, Angel Falls barely makes contact with the cliff over which it flows. It plunges 3,212 feet (979 meters) and is about 500 feet (150 meters) wide at its base. Angel Falls is on the Churún River, located in the Guiana Highlands in southeastern Venezuela.

PANTANAL

The Pantanal is one of the world's largest freshwater wetlands. It is a floodplain in south-central Brazil that extends into northeast Paraguay and southeast Bolivia.

FIVE FAST FACTS

1. The area of the Pantanal varies depending on the season. It ranges from about 54,000 to 81,000 square miles (140,000 to 210,000 square kilometers).

2. The region is home to thousands of varieties of butterflies, hundreds of species of fishes, and some 600 species of birds, including the heron, ibis, duck, greater rhea, and jabiru (a stork).

3. The many mammals and reptiles in the Pantanal include howler monkeys, capuchin monkeys, tapirs, capybaras, anacondas, and caimans.

4. Among the endangered or increasingly rare animals found in the region are the jaguar, giant anteater, cobalt-blue hyacinth macaw (the world's largest parrot), marsh deer, and giant otter.

5. Cattle graze on thousands of acres of ranch land in the Pantanal, and the area is one of Brazil's biggest sources of beef.

NATURAL WONDERS: EUROPE

Sognafjorden.

THE FJORDS OF NORWAY

Much of southern Norway consists of a high plateau penetrated by valleys and fjords, arms of the sea that penetrate inland. The fjords were originally valleys scooped out by glaciers and are very deep. The longest fjord is Sognafjorden, which reaches 127 miles (204 kilometers) inland.

THE GIANT'S CAUSEWAY

On the northern coast of Northern Ireland rises a striking natural formation called the Giant's Causeway, which is made up of thousands of close-fitting columns of basalt rock. There are approximately 40,000 of these stone pillars, each typically with five to seven irregular sides, jutting out of the cliff faces as if they were steps creeping into the sea. The Giant's Causeway formed 50 million to 60 million years ago. It resulted from successive flows of lava inching toward the coast and cooling when they contacted the sea.

MOUNT ETNA

The highest active volcano in Europe is Mount Etna. It rises on the east coast of the island of Sicily. Its topmost elevation is about 11,000 feet (3,350 meters), depending on the effects of its most recent eruption. More than 135 eruptions have been recorded since ancient writers mentioned eruptions 800 years before the Christian era. Etna has been active for more than 2.5 million years.

BLACK FOREST

Many fairy tales originated in the valleys and wooded heights of Germany's Black Forest. Its name (Schwarzwald in German) describes the dark firs and pines that cover the mountainous region. In addition to the fir and pine that predominate, maple, ash, birch, walnut, oak, and beech trees give the landscape a varied color pattern during the autumn. Berries, fruit trees, mushrooms, and heather are common.

THE ROCK OF GIBRALTAR

Near the southern tip of Spain a peninsula forms a finger of land that points to the coast of Africa, 14 miles (23 kilometers) away. That peninsula is the British overseas territory known as Gibraltar. It includes the famous Rock of Gibraltar, which stands at the western gateway to the Mediterranean. The rock is mostly limestone with cliffs and sandy slopes. Its greatest height of 1,396 feet (426 meters) is reached near the southern end.

NATURAL WONDERS: AFRICA

GOLDEN GATE HIGHLANDS NATIONAL PARK

The Golden Gate Highlands National Park lies in the foothills of the Maloti Mountains in South Africa. The park's name comes from the large red and golden sandstone cliffs that rest on either side of the valley leading to the Golden Gate Dam. These cliffs look like a golden gate when viewed in bright sunlight. Golden Gate Highlands National Park protects a large grassland area and the animals that live there. The park provides a refuge for some of South Africa's rarest birds.

GREAT RIFT VALLEY

The longest rift on Earth's surface, the Great Rift Valley is a long, deep depression with steep, wall-like cliffs, extending from Jordan in southwestern Asia southward through Africa to Mozambique. The rift has a total distance of approximately 4,000 miles (6,400 kilometers) and an average width of 30 to 40 miles (50 to 65 kilometers). It is a continental extension of the midoceanic ridge system, a generally submerged mountain range encircling the globe.

Lake Nakuru, one of the saline lakes of the lake system lying in the Great Rift Valley of eastern Africa, is primarily known for its many species of birds, including vast numbers of pink flamingos.

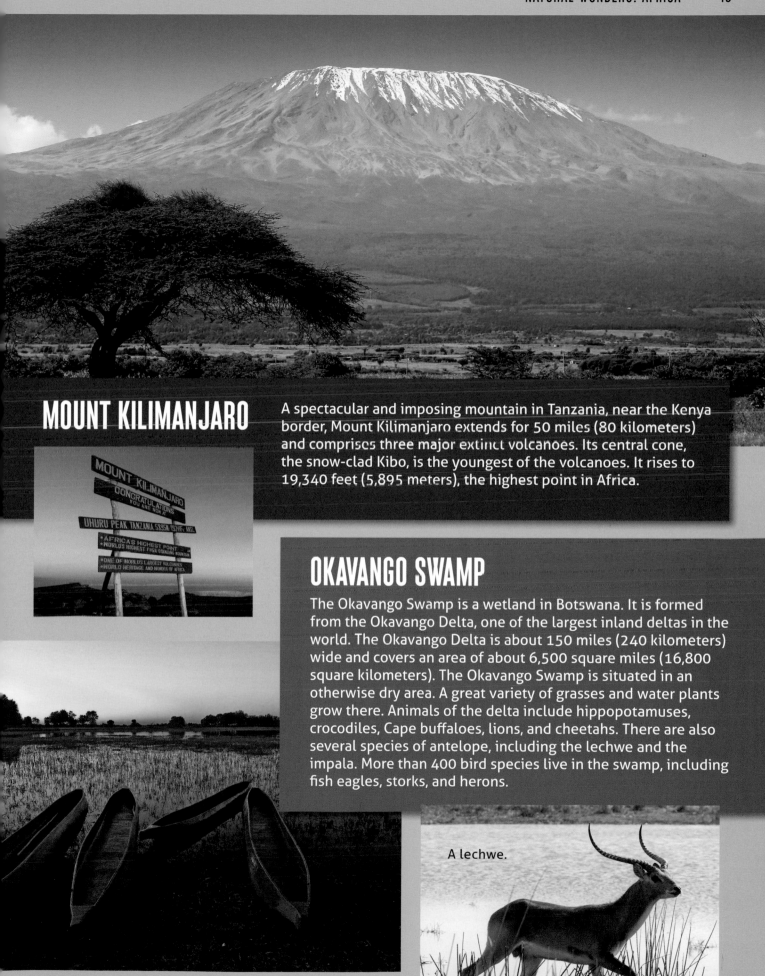

MOUNT KILIMANJARO

A spectacular and imposing mountain in Tanzania, near the Kenya border, Mount Kilimanjaro extends for 50 miles (80 kilometers) and comprises three major extinct volcanoes. Its central cone, the snow-clad Kibo, is the youngest of the volcanoes. It rises to 19,340 feet (5,895 meters), the highest point in Africa.

OKAVANGO SWAMP

The Okavango Swamp is a wetland in Botswana. It is formed from the Okavango Delta, one of the largest inland deltas in the world. The Okavango Delta is about 150 miles (240 kilometers) wide and covers an area of about 6,500 square miles (16,800 square kilometers). The Okavango Swamp is situated in an otherwise dry area. A great variety of grasses and water plants grow there. Animals of the delta include hippopotamuses, crocodiles, Cape buffaloes, lions, and cheetahs. There are also several species of antelope, including the lechwe and the impala. More than 400 bird species live in the swamp, including fish eagles, storks, and herons.

A lechwe.

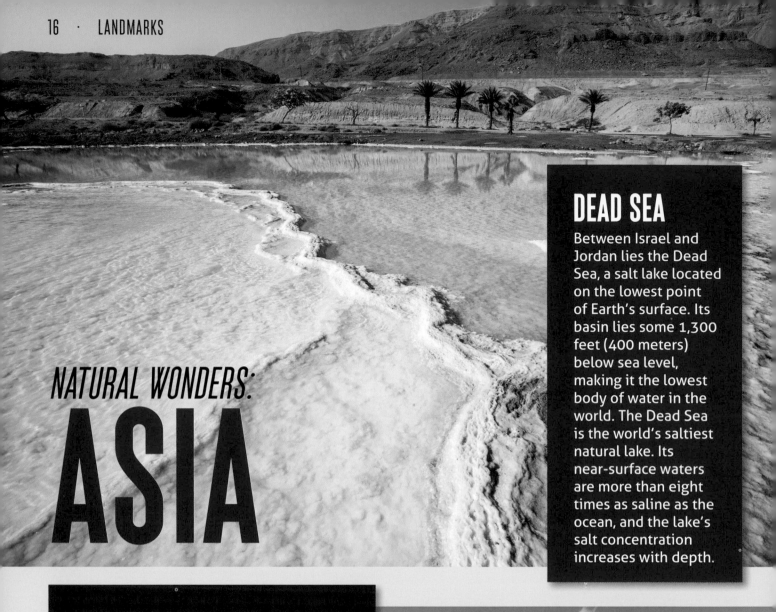

NATURAL WONDERS:
ASIA

DEAD SEA

Between Israel and Jordan lies the Dead Sea, a salt lake located on the lowest point of Earth's surface. Its basin lies some 1,300 feet (400 meters) below sea level, making it the lowest body of water in the world. The Dead Sea is the world's saltiest natural lake. Its near-surface waters are more than eight times as saline as the ocean, and the lake's salt concentration increases with depth.

THE HIMALAYAS AND EVEREST

The highest mountain range on Earth, the Himalayas form the northern border of the Indian subcontinent in Asia. The mountains extend in a massive arc for about 1,550 miles (2,500 kilometers) from west to east with more than 30 peaks rising to heights greater than 24,000 feet (7,300 meters) above sea level. These include Mount Everest, the world's highest peak at 29,035 feet (8,850 meters), Kanchenjunga at 28,208 feet (8,598 meters), Makalu at 27,766 feet (8,463 meters), and Dhaulagiri at 26,810 feet (8,172 meters). The Sanskrit name Himalayas, meaning "abode of snow," truly characterizes the vast permanent snowfields above the snow line. These mountains pose the greatest challenge in the world to mountaineers.

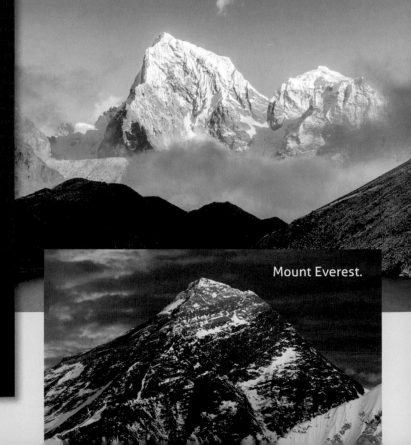

Mount Everest.

GOBI

The Mongolian word *gobi* means "waterless place," and it has become the name for a large desert and semidesert region of Central Asia. The Gobi stretches across vast areas of southern Mongolia and northern China. Contrary to the popular image of deserts as being sandy, most of the Gobi consists of bare rock. The climate of the Gobi is continental: Winter is cold and severe, spring is dry and cold, and summer is warm. Temperatures range from average lows of −40°F (−40°C) in January to average highs of 113°F (45°C) in July. A very dry region, the Gobi has a total annual precipitation that varies from fewer than 2 inches (5 centimeters) in the west to more than 8 inches (20 centimeters) in the northeast.

KRAKATOA

The volcano Krakatoa (also spelled Krakatau) is located on Rakata, an island in the Sunda Strait between Java and Sumatra, Indonesia. Its eruption in 1883 was one of the most catastrophic ever witnessed in recorded history.

NATURAL WONDERS: AUSTRALIA

Spinifex grass in the Great Victoria Desert.

DARLING RIVER

The longest river in Australia is the Darling River, at a length of 1,702 miles (2,739 kilometers). It is the largest tributary of the Murray River, the country's principal river. Much of the Darling's course runs through dry land—extensive saltbush pastures that receive an average of less than 10 inches (25 centimeters) of rain annually. For this reason, the river often loses more water by evaporation than it gains from its tributaries, many of which sometimes fail to reach the main stream.

There are 21 native species of fish in the Darling River. The river is also home to hundreds of species of invertebrates and many mammals, birds, and amphibians. Plant species include saltbush, bluebush, and acacia.

The place where the Darling and Murray Rivers join.

GREAT VICTORIA DESERT

An immense dry area known as the Great Victoria Desert stretches across southern Australia. It covers an area of about 250,000 square miles (647,000 square kilometers). Most of the desert consists of a vast expanse of sand dunes, though in some places a layer of tightly packed pebbles covers the ground.

Grass of the genus *Triodia (Spinifex)* grows in parts of the desert, and there are also scattered acacia trees and shrubs. Wildlife includes reptiles such as skinks, geckos, monitor lizards, and copperhead snakes as well as mice, dingoes, and foxes.

ULURU

One of Australia's most famous landmarks, Uluru/Ayers Rock is a giant mass of weathered sandstone located in the southwestern part of the Northern Territory.

FIVE FAST FACTS

1. It is of great cultural significance, as shallow caves at the base of the rock are sacred to several Aboriginal tribes. Within the caves are many Aboriginal carvings and paintings.

2. Uluru/Ayers Rock is composed of a type of coarse-grained sandstone known as arkose.

3. The rock appears in different shades of pinks, reds, oranges, and browns depending on the position of the sun. At sunset it is a fiery orange-red.

4. One of the largest rocks in the world, it rises 1,100 feet (335 meters) above the surrounding desert plain.

5. Over time, rain and wind have eroded the rock, leaving the lower slopes fluted and the top carved by gullies and basins. After rainstorms (which are infrequent in this arid region), the gullies and basins produce large waterfalls.

ANCIENT SITES

ACROPOLIS

Ancient cities were often built around a fortress on top of a hill. When a city spread to the area below, the high part came to be called the acropolis, which means "city at the top" in Greek. The best-known acropolis is in Athens, Greece. The most famous surviving building is the Parthenon. The Parthenon was built almost 2,500 years ago and was dedicated to the goddess Athena.

AJANTA CAVES

Buddhist rock-cut cave temples and monasteries, near Ajanta village, north-central Maharashtra state, western India, are celebrated for their wall paintings depicting colorful Buddhist legends and divinities with an exuberance and vitality that is unsurpassed in Indian art. The temples are hollowed out of granite cliffs on the inner side of a 70-foot (20-meter) ravine in the Wagurna River valley, 65 miles (105 kilometers) northeast of Aurangabad, at a site of great scenic beauty.

EASTER ISLAND STATUES

Far out in the eastern Pacific Ocean, about 2,200 miles (3,500 kilometers) west of Chile, lies Easter Island, one of the loneliest islands in the world. Tourists are drawn to Easter Island by about 900 huge statues called *moai*. The statues are thought to have been carved hundreds of years ago by competing clans of inhabitants. Most of the moai still in existence are from about 1050 to 1680. Each was carved from a single block of soft stone.

NEWGRANGE

An ancient stone monument, Newgrange was built about 3200 BC, during the Neolithic Period, or the New Stone Age. It is located on a ridge in County Meath, Ireland, near the River Boyne. Newgrange is a type of monument known as a passage tomb, a burial place in the shape of a mound over a chamber that is entered by a passage walled with blocks of stone. In addition to its function as a tomb, Newgrange may also have been used as a temple. It is estimated that some 200,000 tons of rock were used to create the monument.

COLOSSEUM

The Colosseum is the giant amphitheater built in Rome under the Flavian emperors. Construction of the Colosseum was begun sometime between AD 70 and 72 during the reign of Vespasian. The amphitheater seated some 50,000 spectators, who were shielded from the sun by a massive retractable velarium (awning). The Colosseum was the scene of thousands of hand-to-hand combats between gladiators, of contests between men and animals, and of many larger combats, including mock naval engagements.

PANTHEON

The Pantheon is an ancient Roman building that is renowned for its large concrete dome. Begun in Rome in 27 BC, it was rebuilt AD 118–128 by Emperor Hadrian. Until modern times, the dome was the largest built. It measures about 142 feet (43 meters) in diameter and rises to a height of 71 feet (22 meters) above its base.

PYRAMIDS

In the 26th century BC, as Egyptian civilization was reaching its height, three kings—Khufu, his son Khafre, and his grandson Menkure—ordered the construction of three huge pyramids that would serve as their tombs. The first of these, the Great Pyramid, is the largest ever built. It stands with the other two pyramids and the Great Sphinx in a cluster near the town of Giza. The ancient Greeks named the pyramids one of the Seven Wonders of the World, and today they are the only one of those wonders that still exists.

THE GREAT SPHINX

The Great Sphinx at Giza was carved about 2500 BC. It stands near the three great pyramids, gazing across the Nile River, to the east. The head is believed to be a portrait of Khafre, a pharaoh of the Old Kingdom, who ruled during the 4th dynasty (about 2575 to 2465 BC). It is thought that a temple stood between the legs and that Egyptians came here to worship the rising sun.

FIND OUT MORE ABOUT PYRAMID BUILDING IN THE VR APP!

STONEHENGE

The prehistoric monument known as Stonehenge includes a circular arrangement of massive, upright stones surrounded by a large circular earthen embankment. It was built between about 3100 and 1500 BC and is located about 8 miles (13 kilometers) northwest of Salisbury, in southern England. Stonehenge is believed to have been a place of worship of some kind.

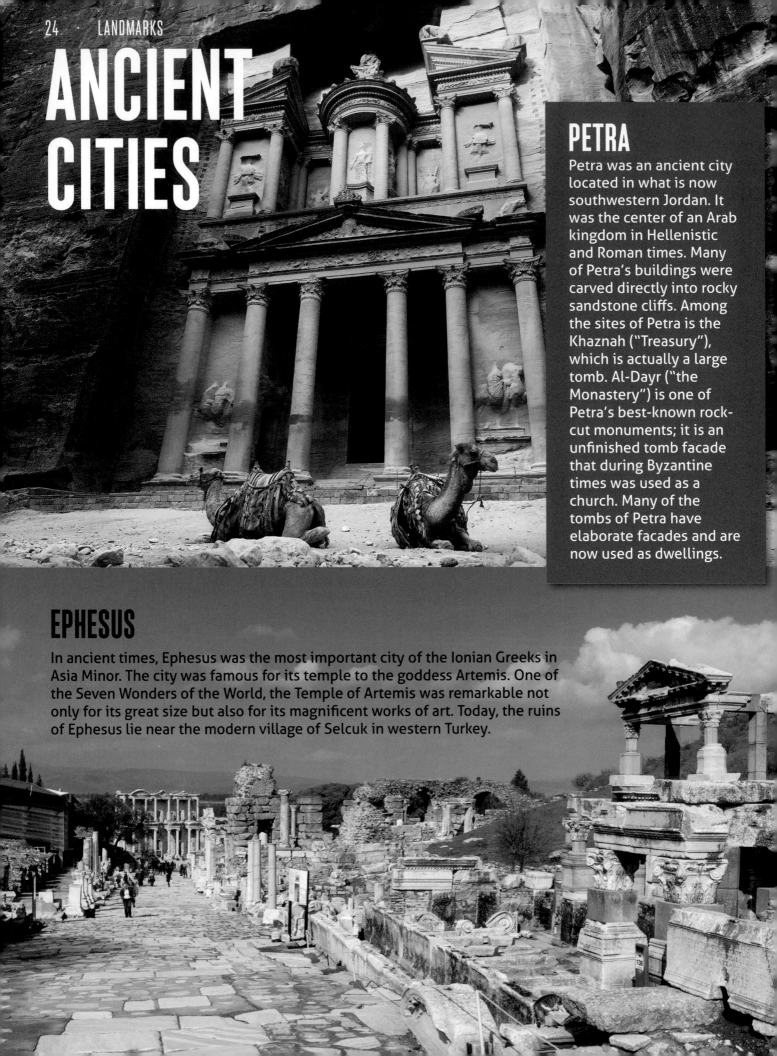

ANCIENT CITIES

PETRA

Petra was an ancient city located in what is now southwestern Jordan. It was the center of an Arab kingdom in Hellenistic and Roman times. Many of Petra's buildings were carved directly into rocky sandstone cliffs. Among the sites of Petra is the Khaznah ("Treasury"), which is actually a large tomb. Al-Dayr ("the Monastery") is one of Petra's best-known rock-cut monuments; it is an unfinished tomb facade that during Byzantine times was used as a church. Many of the tombs of Petra have elaborate facades and are now used as dwellings.

EPHESUS

In ancient times, Ephesus was the most important city of the Ionian Greeks in Asia Minor. The city was famous for its temple to the goddess Artemis. One of the Seven Wonders of the World, the Temple of Artemis was remarkable not only for its great size but also for its magnificent works of art. Today, the ruins of Ephesus lie near the modern village of Selcuk in western Turkey.

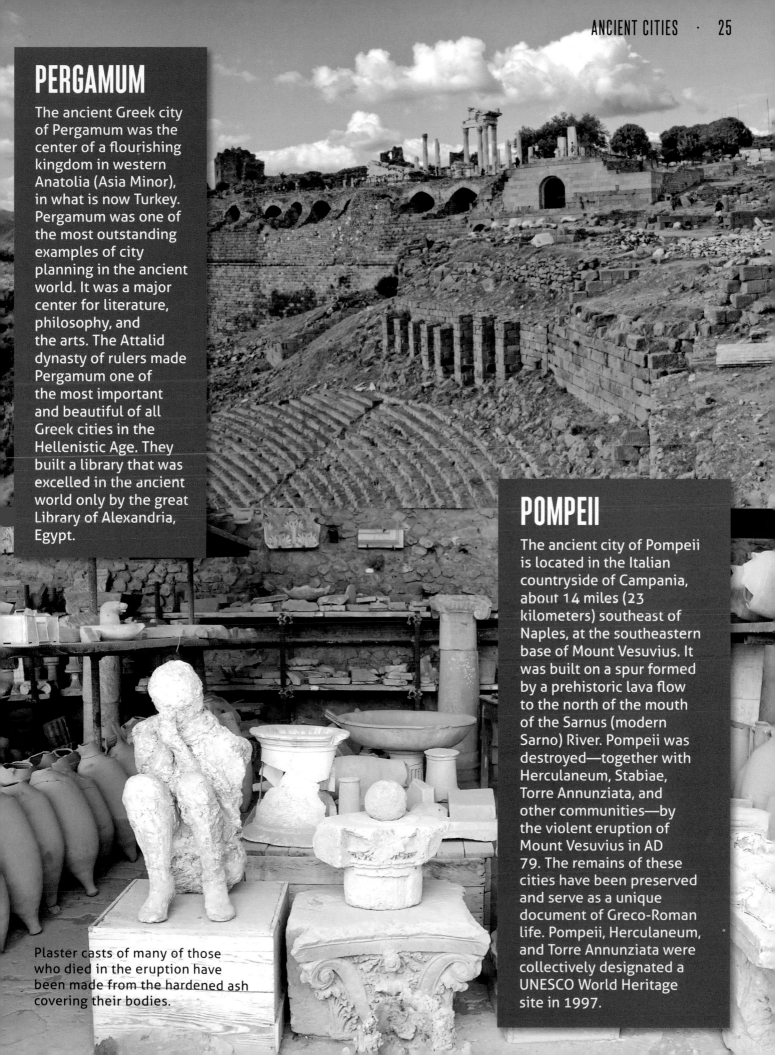

PERGAMUM

The ancient Greek city of Pergamum was the center of a flourishing kingdom in western Anatolia (Asia Minor), in what is now Turkey. Pergamum was one of the most outstanding examples of city planning in the ancient world. It was a major center for literature, philosophy, and the arts. The Attalid dynasty of rulers made Pergamum one of the most important and beautiful of all Greek cities in the Hellenistic Age. They built a library that was excelled in the ancient world only by the great Library of Alexandria, Egypt.

POMPEII

The ancient city of Pompeii is located in the Italian countryside of Campania, about 14 miles (23 kilometers) southeast of Naples, at the southeastern base of Mount Vesuvius. It was built on a spur formed by a prehistoric lava flow to the north of the mouth of the Sarnus (modern Sarno) River. Pompeii was destroyed—together with Herculaneum, Stabiae, Torre Annunziata, and other communities—by the violent eruption of Mount Vesuvius in AD 79. The remains of these cities have been preserved and serve as a unique document of Greco-Roman life. Pompeii, Herculaneum, and Torre Annunziata were collectively designated a UNESCO World Heritage site in 1997.

Plaster casts of many of those who died in the eruption have been made from the hardened ash covering their bodies.

BABYLON

On the Euphrates River, in the land that is now Iraq, ruins of the world's first great city stand alone in the desert. The city bore the proud name Bab-Ilu, meaning "gate of the gods." During the first thousand years of its known history, Babylon was a mere village. It became the capital of the kingdom of Babylon about 1894 BC and reached its first peak of glory in the reign of Hammurabi, the lawgiver.

VIJAYANAGAR

Vijayanagar (or Vijayanagara) was the name of a great ruined city in southern India as well as the name of the powerful Hindu empire that ruled from the city. Vijayanagar means "City of Victory" in Sanskrit. The city of Vijayanagar and the first dynasty of the Vijayanagar kingdom were founded in 1336. As the capital of a great empire, the city of Vijayanagar was a symbol of vast power and wealth, with thriving trade and impressive architecture. It had palaces, numerous Hindu temples and shrines, fortifications, markets, roads, canals, wells, and houses. The empire gradually dissolved, ending about 1614.

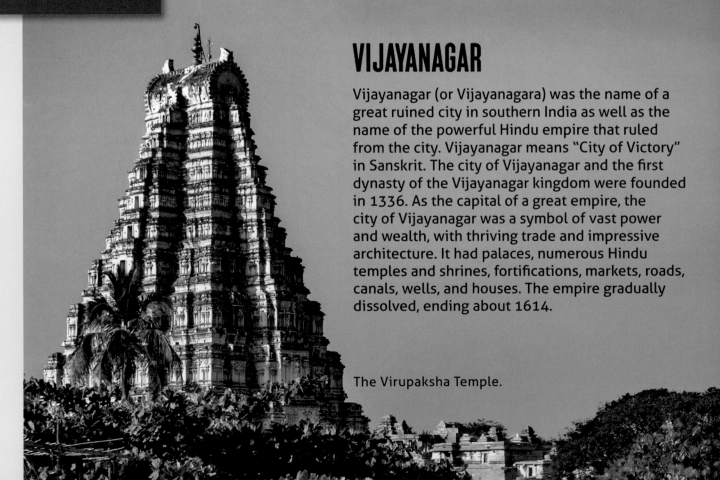

The Virupaksha Temple.

MOHENJO-DARO

The largest city of the ancient Indus Valley civilization was Mohenjo-daro, located on the right bank of the Indus River, in what is now southeastern Pakistan. The civilization existed from about 2500 BC to 1700 BC on the Indian subcontinent. Mohenjo-daro is a remarkable example of ancient urban planning. Artificial barriers were built around the city to protect it from the Indus River.

GREAT ZIMBABWE:
FIVE FAST FACTS

1 Ideally situated between the goldfields of what is now Zimbabwe and the coast of modern Mozambique, the city of Great Zimbabwe gradually evolved from a prosperous farming community into the center of a thriving trading state.

2 The Great Zimbabwe civilization reached its height in the 14th and early 15th centuries, when the capital had a population of 15,000 to 20,000.

3 Owing to taxes on trade and tribute from chiefdoms, the kings of Zimbabwe lived in luxury, surrounded by gold and copper accoutrements and exotic imports, such as beads, porcelain, and cloth, from China, Persia, and India.

4 The ruins of Great Zimbabwe attest to the stone-working skills of the region's inhabitants, the ancestors of the present-day Shona people. (The name Zimbabwe is a Shona word meaning "stone houses.")

5 Without the use of mortar, artisans crafted elaborate stone structures with walls that sometimes stood taller than 30 feet (9 meters).

MESA VERDE

Mesa Verde National Park in southwestern Colorado contains hundreds of pueblo (Indian village) ruins that are up to 13 centuries old. The most striking pueblos are multistoried apartments built under overhanging cliffs. The largest cliff dwelling in the park is Cliff Palace, which housed as many as 250 people in its 217 rooms and 23 kivas (underground ceremonial rooms).

TEOTIHUACÁN

Located near present-day Mexico City, Teotihuacán was the greatest city of the Americas before the arrival of Europeans. At its height in about AD 500, it covered some 8 square miles (20 square kilometers) and may have housed more than 150,000 people. At the time it was one of the largest cities in the world. It was the region's major economic as well as religious center. The city contained great plazas, temples, palaces of nobles and priests, and some 2,000 single-story apartment compounds.

TIKAL

A city and ceremonial center of the ancient Maya civilization, Tikal was the largest urban center in the southern Maya lowlands. It stood in a tropical rainforest, 19 miles (30 kilometers) north of Lake Petén Itzá in what is now the northern part of the region of Petén, Guatemala. Tikal flourished about AD 600–900. During this period its great plazas, pyramids, and palaces were built, and Maya art flowered in monumental sculpture and vase painting. The site's major buildings include five pyramid-shaped temples. The highest of them is Pyramid IV, which rises to 213 feet (65 meters). It is one of the tallest structures in the Western Hemisphere that was created before the arrival of Europeans in the late 15th century.

 SEE PYRAMID IV IN THE VR APP!

CHICHÉN ITZÁ

The ruined ancient Mayan city of Chichén Itzá is located in southeastern Mexico, in the state of Yucatán. Founded in about the 6th century AD, it declined in importance with the rise of the Mayan city of Mayapán in about 1200. Among its ruins are many monumental stone buildings, richly ornamented with relief sculptures and Mayan hieroglyphics.

MACHU PICCHU

The Andes Mountains of Peru feature the ruins of many cities built by the Inca people. The most famous of these is Machu Picchu, located in south-central Peru about 50 miles (80 kilometers) northwest of the city of Cuzco, the capital of the Inca empire. The dwellings at Machu Picchu were probably built and occupied from the mid-1400s to the early or mid-1500s. Most of the white granite structures at Machu Picchu are very well preserved because of the quality of Incan engineering and stonework.

PLACES OF WORSHIP

The first church buildings at Clonmacnoise were made out of timber and have not survived, but—from about 900—stone was used for construction. The ruins of stone churches, known as the Seven Churches of Clonmacnoise, and two 12th-century towers still survive and are protected as part of a national monument.

CLONMACNOISE

The earliest and foremost Irish monastic city was Clonmacnoise, a Christian center on the left bank of the River Shannon, in County Offaly, central Ireland. Clonmacnoise was established about 545, when St. Ciaran founded an abbey there. By the 9th century Clonmacnoise had become an important center of learning, and several books of annals were compiled there. The cathedral, or Great Church, was founded about 900 and was rebuilt in the 14th century.

LALIBELA

The town of Lalibela, in north-central Ethiopia, is famous for its 11 Coptic Christian church buildings. Each of the 11 churches was carved out of solid rock about 800 years ago. The rock churches of Lalibela were built underground.

The Church of St. George at Lalibela.

HOLY SEPULCHRE

The tomb in Jerusalem in which Jesus was buried is known as the Holy Sepulchre. It is also the name of the church built on the traditional site of his Crucifixion and burial. According to the Bible, the tomb was close to the place of the Crucifixion, and so the Church of the Holy Sepulchre was planned to enclose the site of both cross and tomb. The church is a major site of Christian pilgrimage.

ST. PETER'S BASILICA

In the Roman Catholic religion, a basilica is a church of special importance. St. Peter's is built on the site of a 4th-century basilica that is believed to enclose the tomb of St. Peter, the founder of the church. The present structure was consecrated in 1626 after more than a century of building. Notable architects directed the construction. Among them were Donato Bramante, Raphael, and, perhaps most important, Michelangelo. Michelangelo designed the great dome, which rises 390 feet (119 meters) above the floor. Many celebrated Renaissance artists contributed to the rich ornamentation of the interior.

YAMOUSSOUKRO BASILICA

Yamoussoukro Basilica is a Roman Catholic church in Yamoussoukro, Côte d'Ivoire, Africa. Built between 1986 and 1989, it is the largest Christian church building in the world. The Yamoussoukro Basilica was modeled on Saint Peter's Basilica, the church of the popes, in Vatican City. The basilica can hold 18,000 worshipers. There is space for another 300,000 people outside.

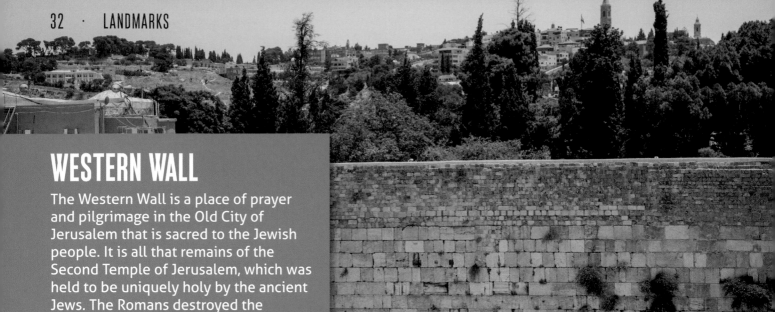

WESTERN WALL

The Western Wall is a place of prayer and pilgrimage in the Old City of Jerusalem that is sacred to the Jewish people. It is all that remains of the Second Temple of Jerusalem, which was held to be uniquely holy by the ancient Jews. The Romans destroyed the Temple in AD 70. The authenticity of the Western Wall has been confirmed by tradition, history, and archaeological research. The wall dates from about the 2nd century BC, though its upper sections were added at a later date.

TOURO SYNAGOGUE

Touro Synagogue, in Newport, Rhode Island, is the oldest synagogue in the United States. It was founded by Spanish and Portuguese Jews in 1763 and designated a national historic site in 1946.

CAPERNAUM SYNAGOGUE

Capernaum, to the northwest of the Sea of Galilee in northern Israel, has preserved one of the most beautiful Jewish synagogues in the area, dating back to the 2nd and 3rd centuries.

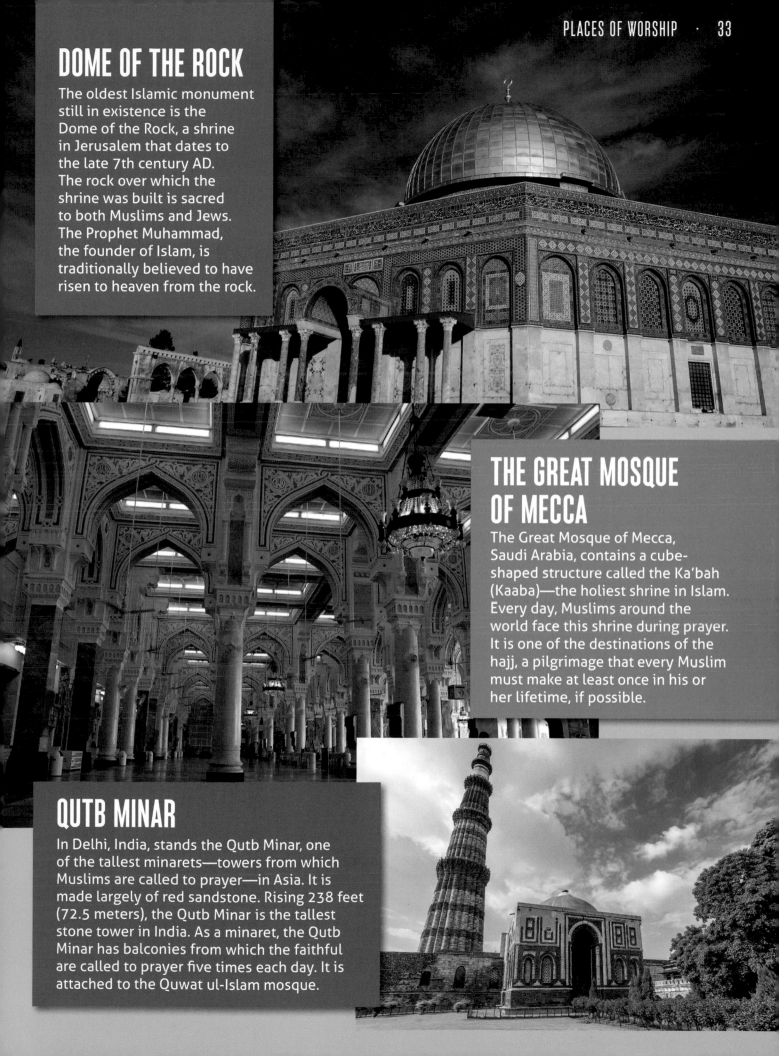

DOME OF THE ROCK

The oldest Islamic monument still in existence is the Dome of the Rock, a shrine in Jerusalem that dates to the late 7th century AD. The rock over which the shrine was built is sacred to both Muslims and Jews. The Prophet Muhammad, the founder of Islam, is traditionally believed to have risen to heaven from the rock.

THE GREAT MOSQUE OF MECCA

The Great Mosque of Mecca, Saudi Arabia, contains a cube-shaped structure called the Ka'bah (Kaaba)—the holiest shrine in Islam. Every day, Muslims around the world face this shrine during prayer. It is one of the destinations of the hajj, a pilgrimage that every Muslim must make at least once in his or her lifetime, if possible.

QUTB MINAR

In Delhi, India, stands the Qutb Minar, one of the tallest minarets—towers from which Muslims are called to prayer—in Asia. It is made largely of red sandstone. Rising 238 feet (72.5 meters), the Qutb Minar is the tallest stone tower in India. As a minaret, the Qutb Minar has balconies from which the faithful are called to prayer five times each day. It is attached to the Quwat ul-Islam mosque.

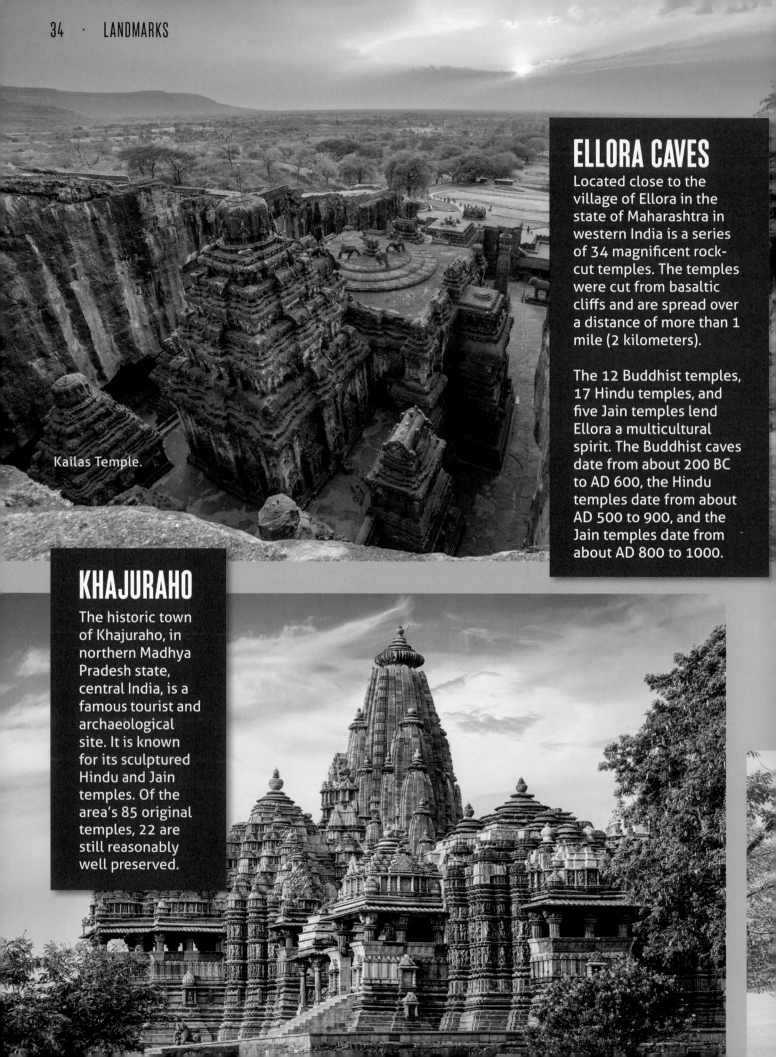

Kailas Temple.

ELLORA CAVES

Located close to the village of Ellora in the state of Maharashtra in western India is a series of 34 magnificent rock-cut temples. The temples were cut from basaltic cliffs and are spread over a distance of more than 1 mile (2 kilometers).

The 12 Buddhist temples, 17 Hindu temples, and five Jain temples lend Ellora a multicultural spirit. The Buddhist caves date from about 200 BC to AD 600, the Hindu temples date from about AD 500 to 900, and the Jain temples date from about AD 800 to 1000.

KHAJURAHO

The historic town of Khajuraho, in northern Madhya Pradesh state, central India, is a famous tourist and archaeological site. It is known for its sculptured Hindu and Jain temples. Of the area's 85 original temples, 22 are still reasonably well preserved.

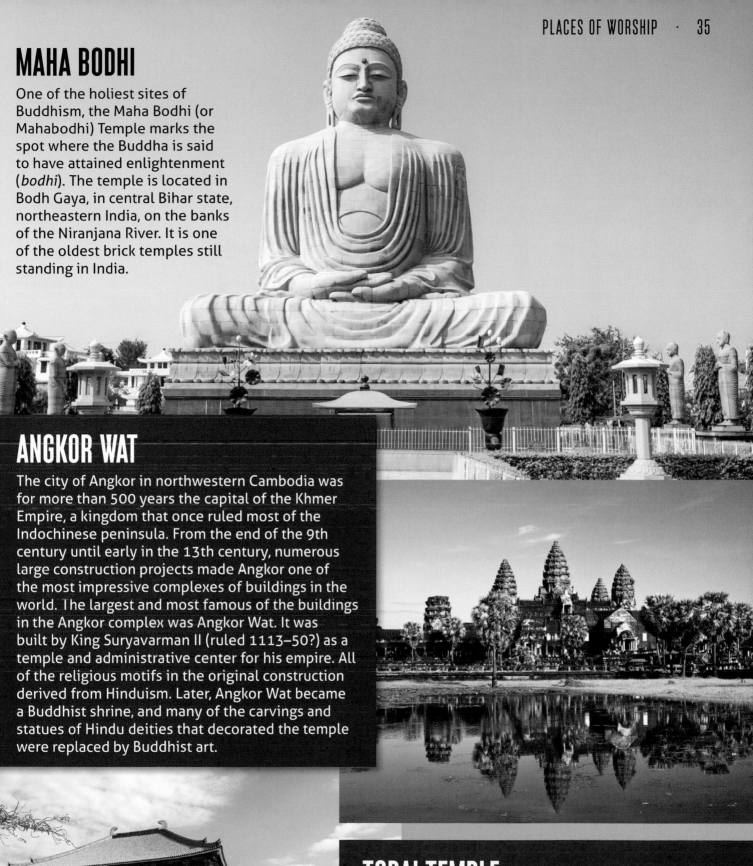

MAHA BODHI

One of the holiest sites of Buddhism, the Maha Bodhi (or Mahabodhi) Temple marks the spot where the Buddha is said to have attained enlightenment (*bodhi*). The temple is located in Bodh Gaya, in central Bihar state, northeastern India, on the banks of the Niranjana River. It is one of the oldest brick temples still standing in India.

ANGKOR WAT

The city of Angkor in northwestern Cambodia was for more than 500 years the capital of the Khmer Empire, a kingdom that once ruled most of the Indochinese peninsula. From the end of the 9th century until early in the 13th century, numerous large construction projects made Angkor one of the most impressive complexes of buildings in the world. The largest and most famous of the buildings in the Angkor complex was Angkor Wat. It was built by King Suryavarman II (ruled 1113–50?) as a temple and administrative center for his empire. All of the religious motifs in the original construction derived from Hinduism. Later, Angkor Wat became a Buddhist shrine, and many of the carvings and statues of Hindu deities that decorated the temple were replaced by Buddhist art.

TODAI TEMPLE

The enormous Todai Temple, in Nara, Japan, is the center of the Kegon sect of Japanese Buddhism. The main buildings were constructed between AD 745 and 752 under the emperor Shomu. Their construction marked the adoption of Buddhism as the national religion of Japan.

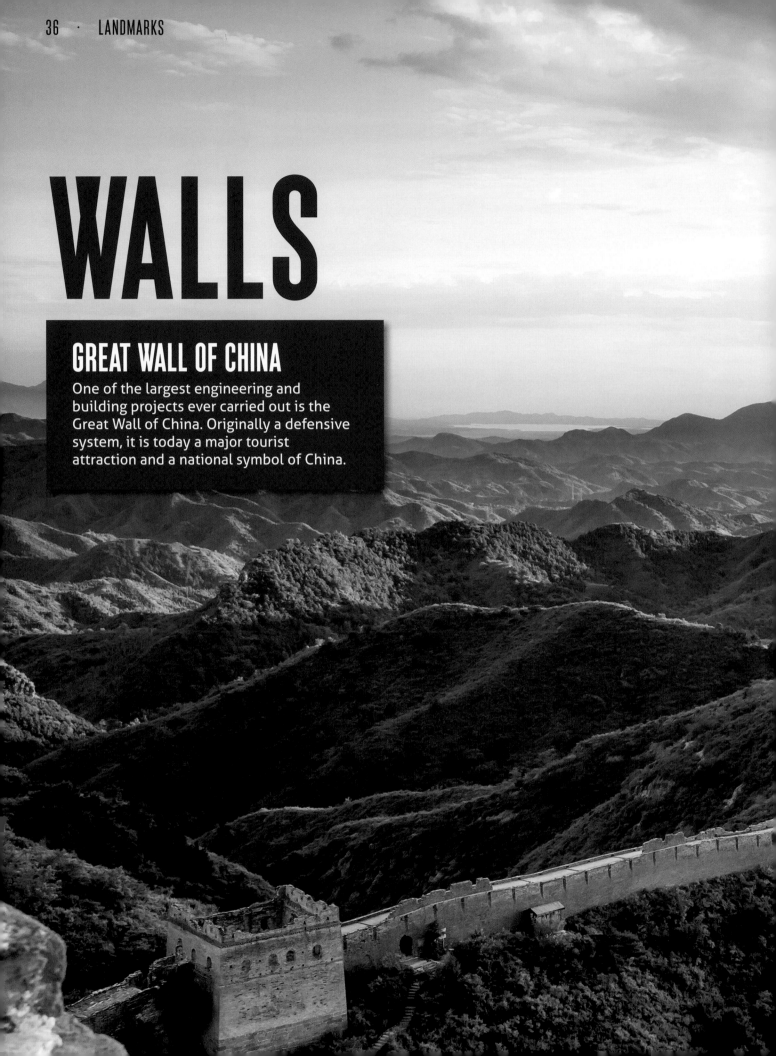

WALLS

GREAT WALL OF CHINA

One of the largest engineering and building projects ever carried out is the Great Wall of China. Originally a defensive system, it is today a major tourist attraction and a national symbol of China.

HADRIAN'S WALL

Hadrian's Wall is a barrier in northern England. It was built by the Roman Empire to keep invaders from the north out of the ancient Roman province of Britain. The wall stretched across the width of northern Britain for 73 miles (118 kilometers) from coast to coast.

The Roman emperor Hadrian went to Britain in 122. He decided to build a stone wall to guard the Romans from the barbarians, or foreign invaders, to the north. Hadrian's Wall was originally designed to be 10 Roman feet wide (with a Roman foot being a bit longer than a standard foot). The width was reduced to between 6 and 8 Roman feet (about 1.8 and 2.4 meters) after two years of construction. The wall was at least 12 feet (about 3.7 meters) high in the eastern section. At every third of a Roman mile there was a tower. At every Roman mile there was a small fort, or fortlet, with a gate, most likely topped with a tower. These towers could hold about 30 soldiers. Larger forts were built on the wall line at roughly 7-mile intervals. Ditches were dug on the north side of the wall.

THE GREAT WALL OF CHINA: FIVE FAST FACTS

1 The Great Wall is actually not one wall but many different walls built over time in northern China and southern Mongolia. Some of the walls run parallel to each other.

2 The most extensive and best preserved version of the wall extends for some 5,500 miles (8,850 kilometers), often tracing the crestlines of hills and mountains as it snakes across the countryside.

3 Roughly 70 percent of the total length is constructed wall. Most of the rest consists of natural barriers such as rivers and mountain ridges, and a small portion consists of ditches and moats.

4 The walls were built over some two millennia.

5 Most of the wall that exists today was built in the 15th and 16th centuries, during the Ming Dynasty, to protect against Mongolian invasions.

DAMS, BRIDGES, AND CANALS

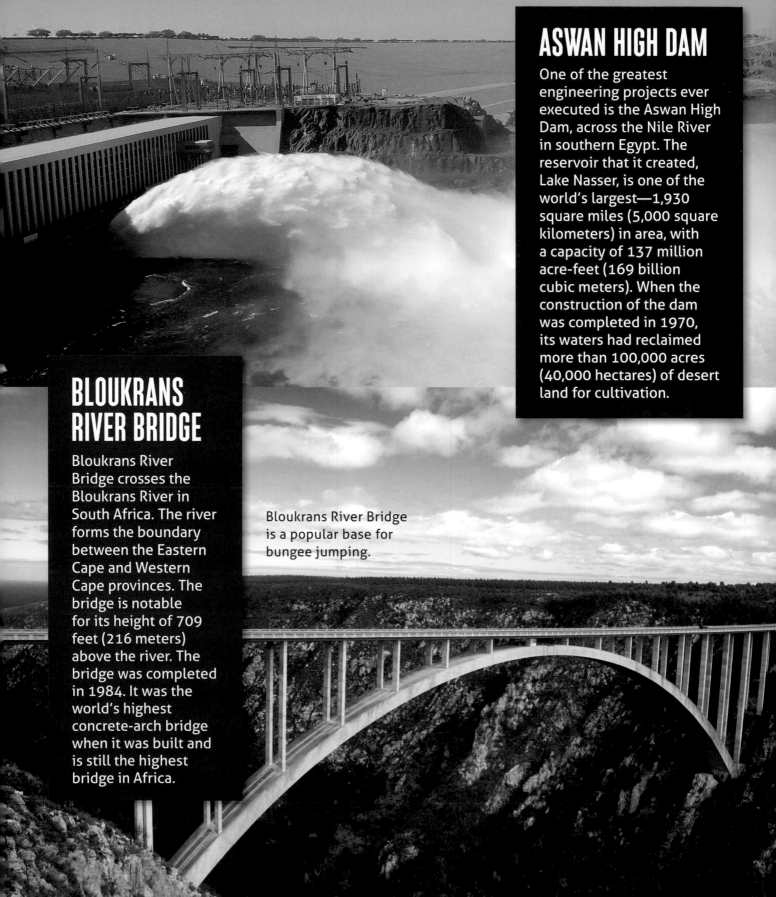

ASWAN HIGH DAM

One of the greatest engineering projects ever executed is the Aswan High Dam, across the Nile River in southern Egypt. The reservoir that it created, Lake Nasser, is one of the world's largest—1,930 square miles (5,000 square kilometers) in area, with a capacity of 137 million acre-feet (169 billion cubic meters). When the construction of the dam was completed in 1970, its waters had reclaimed more than 100,000 acres (40,000 hectares) of desert land for cultivation.

BLOUKRANS RIVER BRIDGE

Bloukrans River Bridge crosses the Bloukrans River in South Africa. The river forms the boundary between the Eastern Cape and Western Cape provinces. The bridge is notable for its height of 709 feet (216 meters) above the river. The bridge was completed in 1984. It was the world's highest concrete-arch bridge when it was built and is still the highest bridge in Africa.

Bloukrans River Bridge is a popular base for bungee jumping.

AKASHI KAIKYO BRIDGE

One of the most impressive feats of modern engineering, the Akashi Kaikyo Bridge in Japan is the longest, tallest, and most expensive suspension bridge ever constructed. It extends 12,828 feet (3,910 meters) across the Akashi Strait, connecting the Kobe metropolitan area on Honshu with Awaji Island. It was designed with a stiffening girder system to withstand earthquakes measuring up to 8.5 on the Richter scale and winds as strong as 179 miles (288 kilometers) per hour.

ERIE CANAL

The Erie Canal is a historic man-made waterway of the United States that is located in New York. It connects Lake Erie at the city of Buffalo in the west-central part of the state with Albany in the east. The 363-mile- (584-kilometer-) long Erie Canal was the first canal in the United States to connect the Great Lakes with the Atlantic Ocean. Construction began in 1817 and was completed in 1825.

A picture of the Erie Canal from 1890.

PANAMA CANAL

The Panama Canal, opened in 1914, links the Atlantic and Pacific oceans. It weaves across a strip of tropical land where the Isthmus of Panama narrows in the shape of a long flattened letter S. The fame of the Panama Canal is not in its size, for it is only about 51 miles (82 kilometers) long. Rather, the canal is an engineering triumph over nature. It has also been a major influence on world trade.

CASTLES, PALACES, FORTS, AND FORTIFICATIONS

In medieval Europe, the castle was a common type of stronghold that provided both protection and living quarters for the king or lord of the land in which it stood. Castles were most common in Europe during the Middle Ages, but similar strongholds have been built in Japan, India, and other countries throughout the world. The castle remained the dominant fortification in western Europe until the 15th century.

The terms castle and palace have often been used interchangeably, but originally they had different purposes. Castles were fortifications, while palaces have been built for centuries solely as royal residences.

WINDSOR CASTLE

The largest inhabited castle in the world is the residence of the British royal family at Windsor, about 22 miles (35 kilometers) west of London. Windsor Castle is not a single building but a large complex of buildings that stretch west to east above the Thames River.

There was a royal residence at Windsor in Saxon times (c. 9th century). William I ("William the Conqueror") developed the present site, constructing a mound with a stockade about 1070. Henry II replaced this with the stone Round Tower, shown here, and added outer walls to the north, east, and south. In the 13th century Henry III completed the south wall and the western end of the lower ward and built a royal chapel on the site of the present-day Albert Memorial Chapel. Edward III made this chapel the center of the newly formed Order of the Garter in 1348 and converted the fortress buildings in the upper ward to residential apartments for the monarchs. These apartments were rebuilt by Charles II and later reconstructed by George IV for use by visitors of state in addition to the monarchs.

TOWER OF LONDON

William, duke of Normandy, conquered England in 1066. One of the first tasks he undertook after becoming King William I was the building of a fortress in the city of London. This structure, called the White Tower, was begun about 1078 and completed several years later by William's son, William II. Today the White Tower stands at the center of an 18-acre (7-hectare) complex of buildings that is called the Tower of London. The tower has served as a fortress, a royal residence, a prison, the royal mint, a public records office, an observatory, a military barracks, a place of execution, and the city zoo. Today it holds the crown jewels and regalia.

The White Tower at the Tower of London.

KRAK DE CHEVALIERS

Krak des Chevaliers is the greatest fortress built by European crusaders in the Middle East. It is located in Syria near the northern border of present-day Lebanon. The fortress is one of the most notable surviving examples of medieval military architecture. It was constructed in the 1100s by a Christian religious-military order called the Knights of the Hospital of St. John (Hospitallers).

THE ALHAMBRA

The Alhambra is a palace and fortress in southern Spain. The large compound was originally home to the Moors who ruled Spain hundreds of years ago. Constructed on a plateau that overlooks the city of Granada, the Alhambra was built chiefly between 1238 and 1358, in the reigns of Ibn al-Ahmar, founder of the Nasrid dynasty, and his successors. After the Moors were expelled from Spain in 1492, much of the interior of the Alhambra was destroyed. Charles V, who ruled in Spain as Charles I (1516–56), rebuilt portions in the Renaissance style.

FORBIDDEN CITY

On Tiananmen Square in the heart of China's capital, Beijing, stands the Forbidden City. Once forbidden to the common people, it is now open as the Palace Museum. The place where 24 of the Ming and Qing emperors lived, it includes a maze of structures with golden-tiled roofs and dark red walls—the colors of the imperial court. In an area of 178 acres (72 hectares) is a complex of palaces, halls, and other buildings that constitutes the largest and most complete existing ensemble of traditional Chinese architecture. The complex was first built from 1406 to 1420, and it remained the seat of the Chinese emperors for nearly 500 years, until the dynastic system collapsed in 1911–12.

AGRA FORT

Agra Fort is a large 16th-century fortress located on the Yamuna River in the historic city of Agra, in Uttar Pradesh state, north-central India. Within its walls lie impressive palace buildings and the beautiful Pearl Mosque. The fort was established by the Mughal emperor Akbar. In its capacity as both a military base and a royal residence, Agra Fort served as the seat of government when the Mughal capital was in Agra. A stretch of parkland and gardens connects the fort to another of Agra's renowned monuments, the Taj Mahal.

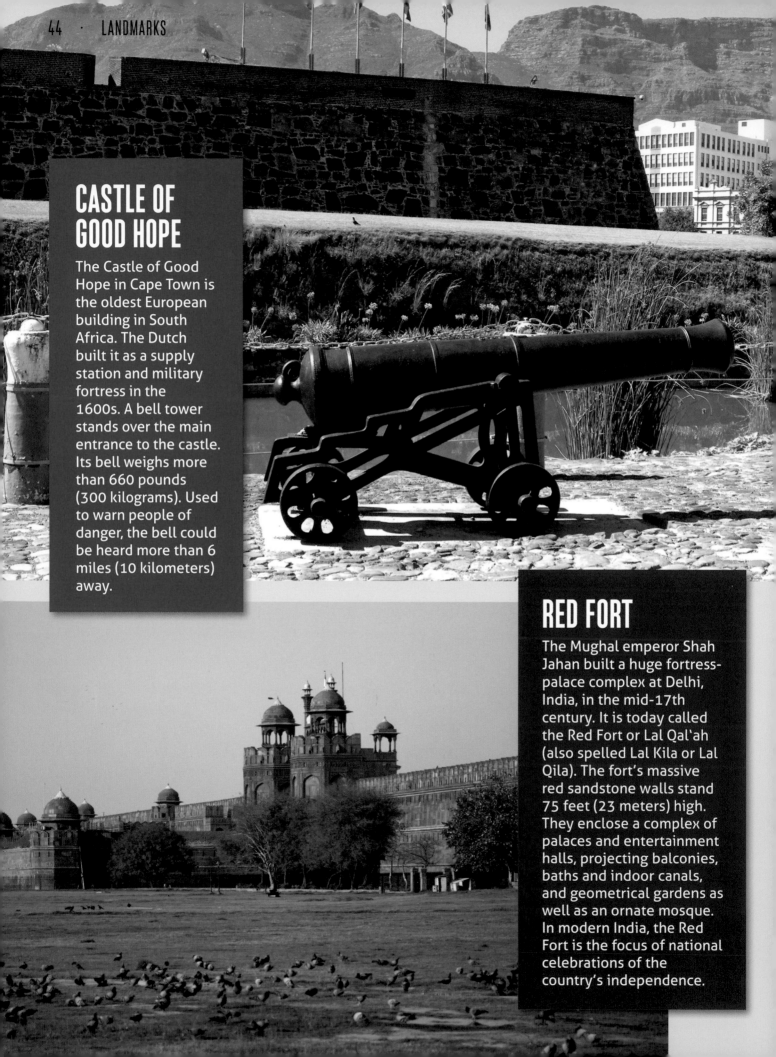

CASTLE OF GOOD HOPE

The Castle of Good Hope in Cape Town is the oldest European building in South Africa. The Dutch built it as a supply station and military fortress in the 1600s. A bell tower stands over the main entrance to the castle. Its bell weighs more than 660 pounds (300 kilograms). Used to warn people of danger, the bell could be heard more than 6 miles (10 kilometers) away.

RED FORT

The Mughal emperor Shah Jahan built a huge fortress-palace complex at Delhi, India, in the mid-17th century. It is today called the Red Fort or Lal Qal'ah (also spelled Lal Kila or Lal Qila). The fort's massive red sandstone walls stand 75 feet (23 meters) high. They enclose a complex of palaces and entertainment halls, projecting balconies, baths and indoor canals, and geometrical gardens as well as an ornate mosque. In modern India, the Red Fort is the focus of national celebrations of the country's independence.

VERSAILLES

13 miles (21 kilometers) southwest of Paris, in the city of Versailles, stands the largest palace in France. It was built because of the consuming envy of King Louis XIV, and once completed it became the object of envy of every other monarch in Europe. Versailles itself served as a royal residence for a little more than a century—from 1682 until 1789, when the French Revolution began.

On August 17, 1661, the French superintendent of finances, Nicolas Fouquet, presided over a large celebration in honor of Louis XIV. The festivities took place at Fouquet's magnificent newly completed château, Vaux-le-Vicomte. When Louis saw this palace he was outraged that one of his ministers should have such a home, while he did not. He had Fouquet thrown into prison and hired the men who had designed and built the palace to do the same for him at Versailles.

BUCKINGHAM PALACE:
FAST FACTS

1 Buckingham Palace is the London residence of the British king or queen.

2 Victoria was the first sovereign to live there (from 1837).

3 The changing of the guard takes place regularly (generally every morning from May through July and every other morning during the rest of the year), but the royal standard is flown over the palace only when the sovereign is in residence.

MONUMENTS

THE LEANING TOWER OF PISA

The Italian city of Pisa is home to the famous bell tower called the Leaning Tower of Pisa. This medieval structure is known for the way it settled, which caused it to lean about 15 feet (4.5 meters) from the perpendicular by the late 20th century. Extensive work was subsequently done to straighten the tower, and its lean was ultimately reduced to about 13.5 feet (4.1 meters).

SEE THE LEANING TOWER OF PISA AND THE TAJ MAHAL IN THE VR APP!

FIVE FAST FACTS

1. Building began in 1173.

2. By the time that three of its eight stories had been completed, however, the uneven settling of the building's foundations in the soft ground became noticeable.

3. At that time, war broke out between the Italian city-states, and construction was halted for almost a century. This pause allowed the tower's foundation to settle and likely prevented its early collapse.

4. The project was plagued with interruptions, as engineers sought solutions to the leaning problem, but the tower was ultimately topped out in the 14th century.

5. In 1990 the tower was closed as engineers undertook a major straightening project. The work was completed in May 2001, and the structure was reopened to visitors later that year. The tower continued to straighten without further excavation, until in May 2008 sensors showed that the motion had finally stopped.

QIN TOMB

The burial place of the ancient Chinese emperor Shihuangdi, the founder of the Qin dynasty, is known as the Qin tomb. Shihuangdi created the first unified Chinese empire and began the construction of the Great Wall of China. Before his death in 210 BC, he had an enormous tomb complex built. It occupies about 20 square miles (50 square kilometers). Today the Qin tomb is a major archaeological site, famous for its thousands of life-size statues of soldiers. Each statue has its own realistic, individually detailed face.

TAJ MAHAL

The Taj Mahal is considered one of the most beautiful buildings in the world. It is located in the city of Agra in northern India. A ruler named Shah Jahan had the Taj Mahal built as a monument and tomb for his beloved wife, Mumtaz Mahal.

Shah Jahan was the Muslim ruler of the Mughal Empire in India from 1628 to 1658. His wife died in 1631, and the construction of the Taj Mahal began the following year.

HUMAYUN'S TOMB

Located in Delhi, India, the 16th-century tomb of the Mughal emperor Humayun is the first of the great masterpieces of Mughal architecture. Built entirely of red sandstone and marble, the tomb shows considerable Persian influence. It introduced high arches and double domes to Indian architecture.

ARC DE TRIOMPHE

The largest triumphal arch in the world, the Arc de Triomphe (in full, Arc de Triomphe de l'Étoile) is one of the best-known commemorative monuments of Paris. The arch is 164 feet (50 meters) high and 148 feet (45 meters) wide. It was initiated by Napoleon Bonaparte and was designed by J.-F.-T. Chalgrin. Construction of the arch began in 1806, though work was not completed until 1836. Decorative relief sculptures celebrating Napoleon's victorious military campaigns were executed on the arch by François Rude, Jean-Pierre Cortot, and Antoine Etex. Beneath the arch lies France's Tomb of the Unknown Soldier.

CHRIST THE REDEEMER

At the top of Mount Corcovado in southeastern Brazil, overlooking Rio de Janeiro, stands a colossal statue of Jesus Christ called Christ the Redeemer. It is the largest Art Deco-style sculpture in the world and is one of Rio de Janeiro's most recognizable landmarks. Construction began on the statue in 1926 and was completed five years later; its dedication was held on October 12, 1931.

The statue stands 98 feet (30 meters) tall, and its horizontally outstretched arms span 92 feet (28 meters).

THE EIFFEL TOWER

When the French government was organizing the Centennial Exposition of 1889, a fair to commemorate the 100th anniversary of the French Revolution, the noted bridge engineer Alexandre-Gustave Eiffel was asked to design and build a structure to symbolize the occasion. His finished product aroused both praise and criticism and a good deal of amazement.

Nothing like it had ever been built. It is a 984-foot (300-meter) tower of open-lattice wrought iron. Not until the Chrysler Building was completed in New York City in 1930 was there a taller structure in the world.

FROM SEA TO SHINING SEA

THE WHITE HOUSE

Where: Pennsylvania Avenue N.W. in Washington, D.C.

When: The cornerstone was laid in 1792.

Fast facts: The office in which the president works is not located in the White House proper. It is in the adjacent West Wing, which was built during the term of Theodore Roosevelt. In 1909, when William Howard Taft was president, the Oval Office was built in the center of the West Wing. In 1934 President Franklin D. Roosevelt had the West Wing enlarged and had the Oval Office relocated to the southeast corner of the wing.

U.S. CAPITOL

Where: Capitol Hill in Washington, D.C.

When: The cornerstone was laid in 1793.

Fast facts: The north wing, containing the Senate chamber, was completed first, and Congress convened there in November 1800. The following year Thomas Jefferson became the first president to be inaugurated at the Capitol, a tradition that has been observed in all subsequent inaugurations.

SEE THE U.S. CAPITOL BUILDING IN THE VR APP!

WASHINGTON MONUMENT

Where: Washington, D.C.

When: 1848; the cornerstone was laid on July 4. Construction was halted at the outbreak of the American Civil War. Some 36 years after construction began, the 3,300-pound (1,500-kilogram) capstone was set on the structure on December 6, 1884.

Fast facts: It is the world's tallest unreinforced all-stone structure, standing 554 feet 7 inches (169 meters) high and weighing an estimated 91,000 tons.

LINCOLN MEMORIAL

Where: Washington, D.C.

When: The cornerstone was set in 1915.

Fast facts: Designed by Henry Bacon on a plan similar to that of the Parthenon in Athens, Greece, the structure is dedicated to "the virtues of tolerance, honesty, and constancy in the human spirit."

STATUE OF LIBERTY

Where: Liberty Island, New York Harbor

When: The statue was dedicated on October 28, 1886.

Fast facts: The figure, formally known as *Liberty Enlightening the World,* is composed of more than 300 copper sheets 3/32 of an inch (2.4 millimeters) thick and weighing a total of 31 tons. It is supported by an iron framework designed by Alexandre-Gustave Eiffel, builder of the Eiffel Tower in Paris.

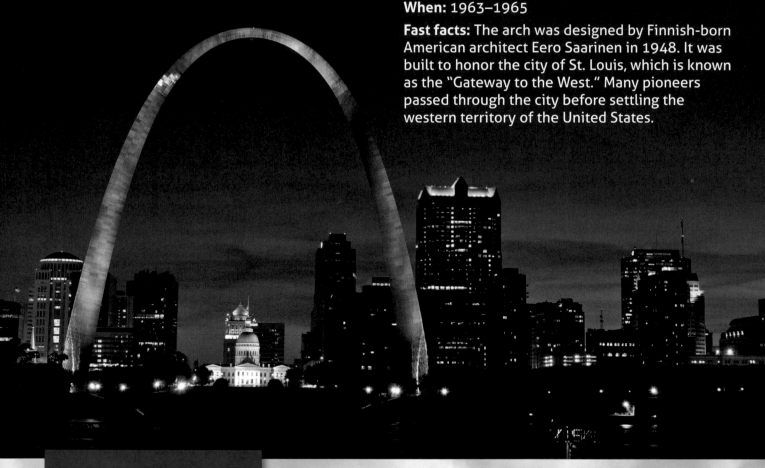

When: 1963–1965

Fast facts: The arch was designed by Finnish-born American architect Eero Saarinen in 1948. It was built to honor the city of St. Louis, which is known as the "Gateway to the West." Many pioneers passed through the city before settling the western territory of the United States.

ALAMO

Where: San Antonio, Texas

When: The Battle of the Alamo during the war for Texas independence from Mexico began on February 22, 1836 when Mexican troops began a siege of the fort.

Fast facts: The siege lasted 13 days. On the morning of March 6, the Mexicans stormed the fort. Nearly all the Alamo defenders were killed. Although the Texan defenders suffered defeat, the siege at the Alamo became for Texans a symbol of heroic resistance.

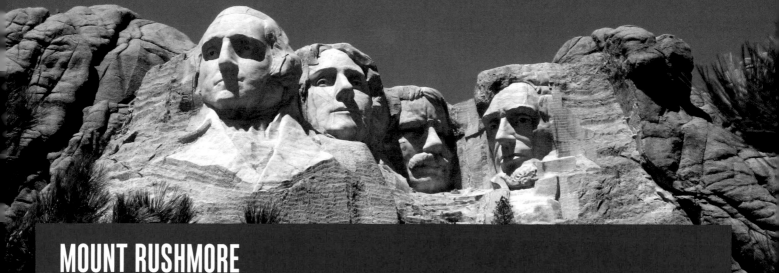

MOUNT RUSHMORE

Where: South Dakota

When: Work on the memorial began in October 1927, shortly after its dedication by President Calvin Coolidge, and continued intermittently for the next 14 years.

Fast facts: In all, the work took six and a half years of actual carving by hundreds of workers, who used dynamite, jackhammers, chisels, and drills to shape the massive stone sculpture. Sculptor Gutzon Borglum's technique involved blasting away much of the rock with explosives, drilling a large number of closely spaced holes, and then chipping at the remaining rock until the surface was smooth. Much of the 450,000 tons of rock removed in the process was left in a pile at the base of the memorial. Washington's head was dedicated in 1930, Jefferson's in 1936, Lincoln's in 1937, and Roosevelt's in 1939.

GOLDEN GATE BRIDGE

Where: San Francisco Bay, California

When: 1933–1937

Fast facts: The main span of the Golden Gate Bridge is 4,200 feet (1,280 meters)—almost a mile long. When it was completed in 1937, it was the longest bridge in the world. It held that record until 1964, when the longer Verrazano-Narrows Bridge opened in New York City.

ARCHITECTURALLY AWESOME

HAGIA SOPHIA

One the world's great buildings, the cathedral of Hagia Sophia in Istanbul, Turkey, is the masterpiece of architecture from the Byzantine Empire. For hundreds of years after its construction (532–37), the Hagia Sophia was the world's largest church. It is an enormous rectangular building capped by a huge main dome with a diameter of nearly 105 feet (32 meters). The dome is supported by curving triangular structures called pendentives as well as by two semidomes.

The monument now standing is essentially the 6th-century structure, though it has been partly rebuilt. An earthquake caused the partial collapse of the dome in 558. It was restored in 562. The dome was rebuilt on a smaller scale after two later partial collapses. The whole church was also reinforced from the outside. It was restored again in the mid-14th century.

SEE THE HAGIA SOPHIA, THE SYDNEY OPERA HOUSE, AND ANOTHER OF OSCAR NIEMEYER'S BUILDINGS, THE CATHEDRAL, IN THE VR APP!

BUILDINGS IN BRASÍLIA BY OSCAR NIEMEYER

Brazilian architect Oscar Niemeyer (1907–2012) was known for his bold, original designs. Many of his works are marked by dramatic geometric images. Niemeyer was particularly noted for his work on Brasília, the capital of Brazil. From 1956 to 1961 Niemeyer designed several buildings in the the newly established capital city. These included the President's Palace, the Brasília Palace Hotel, the Ministry of Justice building, the presidential chapel, and the cathedral.

Presidential Palace.   Brazilian Congress Buildings.   National Museum.

THE SYDNEY OPERA HOUSE

The Sydney Opera House is a concert hall located on Port Jackson (Sydney Harbour), in New South Wales, Australia. Its unique roof, which looks like gleaming white sails, makes it one of the most-photographed buildings in the world. In 1954 the government of New South Wales gave its approval for the building of a musical facility. An international competition was held in 1956 to decide on the design for the building. In January 1957 the judges announced that the winning entry was designed by Danish architect Jørn Utzon.

GARDENS, SQUARES, AND PLAZAS

At the southern end of Red Square is the nine-towered Cathedral of St. Basil the Blessed (originally Church of the Intercession), built 1554–60 to commemorate the defeat of the Tatars (Mongols) of Kazan and Astrakhan by Ivan IV (the Terrible).

RED SQUARE, MOSCOW, RUSSIA

Red Square is an open square in Moscow adjoining the historic fortress and center of government known as the Kremlin. Dating from the late 15th century, just after the Kremlin walls were completed, Red Square has long been a focal point in the social and political history of Russia and the former Soviet Union. Always a market area, the square has also housed, at various times, churches, Moscow's first public library and university, a public theater, and a printing house. Red Square has been the scene of executions, demonstrations, riots, parades, and speeches.

KEW GARDENS, UNITED KINGDOM

Developed from privately owned gardens originating in the 1500s, London's Kew Gardens consists of 300 acres (120 hectares) of botanical gardens, research facilities, and architecturally renowned buildings. Kew Gardens contains some 33,400 taxa of living plants, an Herbarium of approximately seven million dried specimens representing 98 percent of the world's plant genera, and a library of some 130,000 volumes in addition to archived materials, periodicals, and prints and drawings.

TIANANMEN SQUARE, BEIJING, CHINA

Tiananmen Square is one of the largest public squares in the world. It was originally designed and built in 1651.

RYNEK GŁÓWNY, KRAKÓW, POLAND

At the center of the oldest part of Kraków is a square called Rynek Główny (Polish: "Main Square"). On it stands the Gothic church of St. Mary's, the main section of which dates from the late 15th century. Also on the square is the 14th-century Cloth Hall.

PLAZA DE MAYO, BUENOS AIRES, ARGENTINA

The modern city of Buenos Aires developed outward from the Plaza de Mayo, a historic square flanked by the Cabildo (Town Hall) on the western end of the square, which dates from the 18th century, and the Government House, commonly called the Casa Rosada ("Pink House"), on the eastern end.

SKYSCRAPERS

SKYSCRAPERS: **FIVE FAST FACTS**

1 The term *skyscraper* was first used during the 1880s, when the first tall buildings were constructed in the United States.

2 These original skyscrapers were about 10 to 20 stories high.

3 By the late 20th century, however, the term *skyscraper* was used to describe high-rise buildings of unusual height, generally greater than 40 or 50 stories.

4 In the 1860s, steel became widely available in the United States. Since it is stronger and lighter than iron, the use of a steel frame made it possible to construct truly tall buildings.

5 Generally considered the world's first skyscraper, the first building to use steel-girder construction was William Le Baron Jenney's 10-story Home Insurance Company Building (1884–85) in Chicago, Illinois.

 Chicago's Willis Tower. See Willis Tower and Burj Khalifa in the VR App!

CHRYSLER BUILDING

The Chrysler Building's sunburst-patterned stainless steel spire remains one of the most striking features of the Manhattan skyline. Built between 1928 and 1930, the Chrysler Building was briefly the tallest in the world, at 1,046 feet (318.8 meters). It claimed this honor in November 1929—when the building was topped off with a 180-foot (55-metre) spire—and held the record until the Empire State Building opened in 1931.

EMPIRE STATE BUILDING

The Empire State Building, a steel-framed 102-story building completed in New York City in 1931, rises to a height of 1,250 feet (381 meters) and was the first skyscraper of such great vertical dimension. It was the highest structure in the world until 1954.

BURJ KHALIFA

In 1996 the Petronas Twin Towers, in Kuala Lumpur, Malaysia, surpassed the Sears Tower (now Willis Tower) to become the world's tallest buildings. Since then, many skyscrapers have been built in Asia. At 2,717 feet (828 meters), the 162-story Burj Khalifa, in Dubai, United Arab Emirates, was hundreds of feet taller than any other structure when it opened in 2010.

ONE WORLD TRADE CENTER

The title of tallest building in the United States was claimed by One World Trade Center in 2014. The building, initially called Freedom Tower when its design was announced, is 1,776 feet (541 meters) in height.

TEST WHAT YOU KNOW

1. **Which building was built by Shah Jahan?**
   Taj Mahal   Red Fort
   Both

2. **The Pantanal is a wetland in Botswana.**
   True   False

3. **Which mountain chain is longer?**
   Andes   Appalachians

4. **The Acropolis is found in this city.**
   Athens   Rome

5. **The Ajanta Caves are dedicated to this religion.**
   Buddhism   Hinduism

6. **Newgrange and Clonmacnoise are landmarks of this country.**
   England   Ireland   Spain

7. **Angkor Wat is found in this country.**
   Cambodia   India   Pakistan

8. **Which fort was built first?**
   Krak de Chevaliers   Agra Fort

9. **The largest triumphal arch in the world is found in this city.**
   Delhi   Paris   London

10. **These monuments were designed by the same person.**
    Statue of Liberty and Eiffel Tower
    Washington Monument and Gateway Arch
    Versailles and Eiffel Tower

Answers: 1. Both; 2. False; 3. Andes; 4. Athens; 5. Buddhism; 6. Ireland; 7. Cambodia; 8. Krak de Chevaliers; 9. Paris; 10. Statue of Liberty and Eiffel Tower